PAPHNUTIUS & THAIS

Hrotsvitha of Gandersheim

Translated by: D.P. Curtin

Dalcassian Publishing Company
PHILADELPHIA, PA

Copyright @ 2011 Dalcassian Publishing Company

All rights reserved. No part of this publication may be reproduced, distributed, or transmitted in any form or by any means, including photocopying, recording, or other electronic or mechanical methods, without the prior written permission of the publisher, except in the case of brief quotations embodied in critical reviews and certain other non-commercial uses permitted by copyright law. For permission request, write to Dalcassian Publishing Company at dalcassianpublishing at gmail.com

ISBN: 979-8-8689-2059-2 (Paperback)

Library of Congress Control Number:
Author: Curtin, D.P. (1985-)

Printed by Ingram Content Group, 1 Ingram Blvd, La Vergne, Tennessee

First printing edition 2011.

PAPHNATIUS & THAIS

COMEDY.

ARGUMENT.

Conversion of the courtesan Thaïs. The holy monk Paphnutius, following the example of Abraham, goes to find Thaïs under the guise of a lover. He converted her and imposed as penance on her the need to remain confined in a narrow cell for five years. Thaïs by this just expiation is reconciled to the Lord. Fifteen days after having completed her penance, she fell asleep in the bosom of Christ.

INTERLOCUTERS.

PAPHNUCE, hermit. — The DISCIPLES OF PAPHNUTIUS — THAIS. — YOUNG PEOPLE, lovers of THAÏS — ANTOINE and PAUL, hermits. — AN ABBESS.

Scene I.

PAPHNUCE, THE DISCIPLES OF PAPHNUCE.

THE DISCIPLES. —Why this dark face, Paphnutius, our father? Why don't you show us a calm front, as usual?

PAPHNUTIUS. —He whose heart is saddened can only show a gloomy face.

THE DISCIPLES. —What is the cause of your affliction?

PAPHNUTIUS. — The insult we do to the Creator.

THE DISCIPLES. — What insult?

PAPHNUTIUS. — That which he must suffer from his own creature, made in his image.

THE DISCIPLES. —Your words frighten us.

PAPHNUTIUS. — Although the impassive majesty of the Most High cannot be affected by any outrage, nevertheless, if I am permitted to metaphorically attribute to God the sentiments of our weak nature, the most sensible outrage that God can experience is is to see the minor world in revolt against his will, when the major world obeys him without murmuring.

THE DISCIPLES. —What is the minor world?

PAPHNUTIUS. - The man.

THE DISCIPLES. - The man?

PAPHNUTIUS. - Without a doubt.

THE DISCIPLES. - What a man?

PAPHNUTIUS. — Man in general (the human race).

THE DISCIPLES. —How can this be?

PAPHNUTIUS. — This was the will of the Creator.

THE DISCIPLES. - We do not understand.

PAPHNUTIUS. — Indeed, this is not accessible to all minds.

THE DISCIPLES. — Explain this mystery to us.

PAPHNUTIUS. – Listen then.

THE DISCIPLES. — With all the strength of our intelligence.

PAPHNUTIUS. — Just as the major world is made up of four contrary elements, but which by the will of the Creator agree according to the laws of harmony, so man is composed not only of these four elements, but of several other parts which are even more contrary to each other.

THE DISCIPLES. —And what is more contrary than the elements?

PAPHNUTIUS. — The body and the soul; for the elements, although contrary, have one thing in common, which is to be material, whereas the soul is not mortal like the body, nor the spiritual body like the soul.

THE DISCIPLES. - This is true.

PAPHNUTIUS. — However, if we gave in to the reasoning of the dialecticians, we would not agree that the body and the soul are contrary.

THE DISCIPLES. —And who can deny it?

PAPHNUTIUS. — Those who are accustomed to the quibbles of dialectic. Nothing, according to them, is contrary to being, to the ontological substance which is the receptacle of all contraries.

THE DISCIPLES. — What did you mean earlier by this expression: following the laws of harmony?

PAPHNUTIUS. - Here it is. As low and high sounds produce a musical result, if they are united according to harmonic relationships, so dissonant elements form a single world, if they are suitably united.

THE DISCIPLES. — It is astonishing that dissonant things can agree, or that it is possible to call dissonant things concordant.

PAPHNUTIUS. — This is because nothing can be composed of completely similar elements, any more than of elements which have no relation of proportion between them, and which differ entirely in substance and nature.

THE DISCIPLES. — What is music?

PAPHNUTIUS. — One of the sciences of the *quadrivium* of philosophy.

THE DISCIPLES. — What do you call the *quadrivium?*

PAPHNUTIUS. — Arithmetic, geometry, music and astronomy.

THE DISCIPLES. — Why do you call it *quadrivium*?

PAPHNUTIUS. — Because, like a crossroads, from which four paths depart, these four sciences arise directly from one and the same principle of philosophy.

THE DISCIPLES. — We dare not ask you any questions about the three other sciences, because the limited scope of our mind can barely follow the arduous discussion that you have begun.

PAPHNUTIUS. — This matter is, in fact, difficult to understand.

THE DISCIPLES. —Give us only a few superficial notions of the science with which we are concerned at the moment.

PAPHNUTIUS. — I can only tell you about it very briefly, because it is little known to solitary people.

THE DISCIPLES. — What object is she concerned with?

PAPHNUTIUS. - The music?

THE DISCIPLES. - Yes.

PAPHNUTIUS. — It deals with sounds.

THE DISCIPLES. —Are there one or more?

PAPHNUTIUS. — There are three which are so linked together by the analogy of proportions that what is found in one cannot fail to be found in the others.

THE DISCIPLES. —What is the difference between them?

PAPHNUTIUS. — The first is called worldly or celestial, the second human, and the third instrumental.

THE DISCIPLES. — What does celestial consist of?

PAPHNUTIUS. — In the seven planets and the celestial sphere.

THE DISCIPLES. - What do you mean?

PAPHNUTIUS. — Because we find in the planets and in the sphere the same number of intervals, the same degrees and the same consonances as in the strings.

THE DISCIPLES. — What are intervals?

PAPHNUTIUS. — The space between the planets or between the strings.

THE DISCIPLES. — And the degrees?

PAPHNUTIUS. — The same thing as tones.

THE DISCIPLES. — We have no idea of these.

PAPHNUTIUS. — The tone is made up of two sounds: it is proportional to the *epogdous* or *sesquioctave number* (that is to say in the ratio of 9 to 8.)

THE DISCIPLES. — In vain we make all our efforts to understand and quickly overcome your first proposals. You always bring us more difficult ones.

PAPHNUTIUS. — This is inevitable in these kinds of discussions.

THE DISCIPLES. — Tell us something about the consonances, so that at least we know the meaning of this word.

PAPHNUTIUS. — Consonance is a certain harmonic combination.

THE DISCIPLES. - What do you mean?

PAPHNUTIUS. — Because it is composed sometimes of four, sometimes of five, and sometimes of eight sounds.

THE DISCIPLES. — Now that we know that there are three consonances, we would like to know their names.

PAPHNUTIUS. — The first is called *diatessaron*, that is to say *made up of four sounds*; it is in proportion *epitrite* or *sesquitierce* (that is to say in the ratio of 4 to 3). The second is called *diapente or composed of five sounds*; it is in *hemiolar* or *sesqualterous* proportion (that is to say in the ratio of 3 to 2). The third is called *tuning fork*; it is *formed by doubling* (that is to say by the union of the fourth and the fifth) and is composed of eight sounds.

THE DISCIPLES. — Do the sphere and the planets therefore emit sounds, so that we can compare them to strings?

PAPHNUTIUS. — No doubt, and very strong ones.

THE DISCIPLES. —Why don't we hear them?

PAPHNUTIUS. — There are several explanations for this phenomenon. Some think that we cannot hear the sounds of the celestial sphere because of their uninterrupted duration. Others believe it comes from the density of the air. Some believe that such an enormous volume of sound cannot penetrate our narrow ear canal. Some people finally maintain that the sphere produces a sound so sweet, so enchanting, that if men could hear it, they would gather in crowds, neglect all their affairs, and, forgetting themselves, would follow the conductive sound of the east in the west.

THE DISCIPLES. — It's better not to hear it.

PAPHNUTIUS. — The foreknowledge of the Creator judged it thus.

THE DISCIPLES. — That's enough about celestial music; now tell us a few words about human music.

PAPHNUTIUS. —What do you want to know?

THE DISCIPLES. . —What does it consist of?

PAPHNUTIUS. — It consists not only, as I told you, in the union of body and soul, and in the emission of the voice sometimes deep and sometimes high; but we still find it in the regular pulsation of the arteries and in the proportion of certain members, as in the joints of the fingers, which offer us, when we measure them, the same proportions. than those that we have indicated in the consonances; from which it follows that music is not only the harmony of voices, but also that of many other dissimilar things.

THE DISCIPLES. —If we had anticipated that the knot of this question would be so difficult for ignorant people to unravel, we would have preferred to continue not knowing what the minor world is, then to throw ourselves into such difficulties.

PAPHNUTIUS. — No matter the trouble you took, since you now know what was previously unknown to you.

THE DISCIPLES. - It is true; However, we have little taste for philosophical discussions. Our weak minds cannot grasp the subtleties of your untied argument.

PAPHNUTIUS. - You're making fun; I am only an ignoramus; I am not a philosopher.

THE DISCIPLES. —And where did you get this knowledge, the exposition of which we were unable to follow without fatigue?

PAPHNUTIUS. — It is a faint drop that, by chance and without looking for it, I saw, in passing, spring from the abundant sources of science; I collected it, and I wanted to share it with you.

THE DISCIPLES. — We give thanks to your kindness; However, this maxim of the apostle frightens us: "God chooses fools following the world, to shame the so-called wise."

PAPHNUTIUS. —Wise or foolish will deserve to be shamed before the Lord if they do evil.

THE DISCIPLES. - Without a doubt.

PAPHNUTIUS. — All the knowledge that it is possible to have is not what offends God, but the unjust pride of him who knows.

THE DISCIPLES. - This is true.

PAPHNUTIUS. —And for what can science and the arts be more justly and worthily employed than in the praise of Him who created all that we need to know, and who furnishes us with both the material and the instrument science.

THE DISCIPLES. — There is no better use of knowledge.

PAPHNUTIUS. — For the better we know by what admirable law God has regulated the number, the proportion and the balance of all things, the more we burn with love for him.

THE DISCIPLES. — And it is with justice.

PAPHNUTIUS. — But why dwell on this subject, which brings us little pleasure?

THE DISCIPLES. — Tell us the cause of your sadness, so that we do not bear the weight of our curiosity any longer.

PAPHNUTIUS. —When you have heard me, you will have no reason to rejoice.

THE DISCIPLES. — Too often, we know, we find only sorrow at the bottom of satisfied curiosity. However, we cannot overcome ours: it is a fault inherent in human weakness.

PAPHNUTIUS. — An immodest woman came to live in our country.

THE DISCIPLES. — This is a dangerous event for the inhabitants.

PAPHNUTIUS. — This woman, in whom admirable beauty shines, defiles herself with the most horrible impurities.

THE DISCIPLES. — Deplorable misfortune! What's her name?

PAPHNUTIUS. — Thais.

THE DISCIPLES. — Thaïs, the courtesan?

PAPHNUTIUS. - Herself.

THE DISCIPLES. — His infamous life is known to all.

PAPHNUTIUS. — We should not be surprised, because it is not enough for him to run to his ruin with a small number of lovers; she strives to seduce with her charms and lead to their ruin all those who approach her.

THE DISCIPLES. — A disastrous calamity!

PAPHNUTIUS. — Not only do the thoughtless squander with it the little wealth they have left; but the first citizens of the city consume their wealth to enrich it at their expense.

The Disciples. — It makes one shudder with horror.

Paphnutius. — Flocks of lovers flock to her house.

The Disciples. — They lose themselves.

Paphnutius. — These fools, blinded by their desires, are fighting over the entrance to his house. This place resounds with their quarrels.

The Disciples. — Always one vice begets another.

Paphnutius. — Then they come to blows; sometimes they bruise their faces, sometimes they resort to arms, and flood the threshold of this infamous abode with blood.

The Disciples. — Detestable excesses!

Paphnutius. — These are the insults to the Creator over which I cried; you know the cause of my pain.

The Disciples. — It is not without reason that you are distressed, and we have no doubt that the citizens of the heavenly homeland are saddened as you are.

Paphnutius. — What if I were to find her under the guise of a lover? Perhaps I could prevent him from persevering in these disorders?

The Disciples. — May he who poured this design into your soul ensure its success!

Paphnutius. — However, lend me the help of your diligent prayers, so that I do not succumb to the traps of the tempting serpent.

The Disciples. — May he who struck down the king of the dark regions make you triumph over the enemy of humankind!

Scene II.

PAHPHNUCE, THE LOVERS OF THAIS.

PAPHNUTIUS. — I see young people in the forum. I will approach them and ask them where I will find the one I am looking for.

YOUNG PEOPLE. — This stranger seems to want to approach us; let's see what he wants from us.

PAPHNUTIUS. - Hello! young people, who are you?

YOUNG PEOPLE. —Inhabitants of this town.

PAPHNUTIUS. - I salute you.

YOUNG PEOPLE. — Hello to you, whoever you are, foreigner or citizen.

PAPHNUTIUS. - I'm a foreigner.

YOUNG PEOPLE. —And why did you come here? What are you looking for?

PAPHNUTIUS. — I can't say.

YOUNG PEOPLE. - For what?

PAPHNUTIUS. - It's my secret.

YOUNG PEOPLE. —You had better entrust him to us; because, not being from this city, you will have difficulty doing what you want, without the advice of the inhabitants.

PAPHNUTIUS. —Perhaps by telling you what brings me I would raise some obstacles to my plans.

YOUNG PEOPLE. —No obstacle will come from us.

PAPHNUTIUS. — I yield to your promise and trust in your loyalty. I will tell you my secret.

YOUNG PEOPLE. — Do not fear any infidelity on our part or any hindrance to your desires.

PAPHNUTIUS & THAIS

PAPHNUTIUS. — I learned that there lives among you a woman whom everyone is forced to love and who is affable to everyone.

YOUNG PEOPLE. — Do you know his name?

PAPHNUTIUS. - Yes.

YOUNG PEOPLE. — What is her name?

PAPHNUTIUS. — Thais.

YOUNG PEOPLE. — It is the fire that sets all our fellow citizens ablaze.

PAPHNUTIUS. — She is said to be the most beautiful and voluptuous of women.

YOUNG PEOPLE. — Those who spoke to you in this way did not deceive you.

PAPHNUTIUS. — It is for her that I endured a long and difficult journey. I only came to see her.

YOUNG PEOPLE. —There is nothing stopping you from seeing her.

PAPHNUTIUS. — Where does she live?

YOUNG PEOPLE. — Hey, his place is very close.

PAPHNUTIUS. —Is this the house you are pointing at?

YOUNG PEOPLE. - Yes.

PAPHNUTIUS. – I will go.

YOUNG PEOPLE. — If you want, we will accompany you.

PAPHNUTIUS. — I prefer to go alone.

YOUNG PEOPLE. - As you would like.

Scene III.

PAPHNUCE, THAIS.

PAPHNUTIUS. — Are you here, Thaïs, you whom I am looking for?

THAIS. - Who is here? What stranger is talking to me?

PAPHNUTIUS. — A man who loves you.

THAIS. — Whoever loves me is reciprocated.

PAPHNUTIUS. — O Thaïs! Thais! what a long and painful journey I have undertaken to be able to speak to you and contemplate your beauty!

THAIS. - Well! I do not shy away from your gaze, nor refuse to speak with you.

PAPHNUTIUS. — A conversation as intimate as the one I desire requires a more solitary place than the one where we are.

THAIS. — Here is a bedroom, well furnished, and which offers comfortable accommodation.

PAPHNUTIUS. — Is there not a more secluded place where we can talk more secretly?

THAIS. — Yes, there is still a more remote place in this house, and so secret that after me only God knows it.

PAPHNUTIUS. — Which god?

THAIS. — The true God.

PAPHNUTIUS. — So, you believe that God knows everything?

THAIS. — I know that nothing is hidden from him.

PAPHNUTIUS. — Do you believe that it is indifferent to the actions of sinners, or that on the contrary it is equitable for all?

THAIS. — I am convinced that, in the scales of his justice, he weighs the actions of all men, and that he dispenses to each, according to his works, punishment and reward.

PAPHNUTIUS. — O Jesus Christ! How admirable and patient is your kindness to us! Even those whom you see knowingly sinning, you delay in punishing them!

THAIS. —Why are you changing color? Why are you shaking? Why are you shedding tears?

PAPHNUTIUS. —Your presumption horrifies me, I deplore your fall; for you knew these truths, and yet you have lost so many souls!

THAIS. —Woe, woe is me!

PAPHNUTIUS. — You will be damned with all the more justice as you have, with greater presumption, knowingly offended the divine majesty!

THAIS. — Alas! alas! What do you say? What threats do you make to a poor unfortunate woman?

PAPHNUTIUS. — The torments of hell await you, if you persevere in crime.

THAIS. —The severity of your reprimands shakes the last recesses of my frightened heart.

PAPHNUTIUS. — Would to God that fear penetrated to the depths of your bowels! You would no longer have the audacity to indulge in dangerous pleasures.

THAIS. —And what place can there be left now for corrupt pleasures in a heart where bitter repentance reigns supreme and the terror inspired in me by crimes the enormity of which my conscience knows?

PAPHNUTIUS. — What I want above all is that, freeing yourself from the thorns of vice, you shed a tear of compunction over your faults.

THAIS. —Ah! if you could believe, ah! if you could hope that a sinner soiled, as I am, by the mire of a thousand and a thousand impurities, could still atone for her crimes and merit her forgiveness through a penance, however harsh it may be!...

PAPHNUTIUS. — There is no sin so serious, no crime so enormous, that cannot be expiated by the tears of repentance, provided that works prove its sincerity.

THAIS. — Teach me, I pray you, my father, by what works I can obtain the favor of my reconciliation.

PAPHNUTIUS. — Despise the century and flee the company of your dissolute lovers.

THAIS. —And what should I do next?

PAPHNUTIUS. — Retire to a solitary place, where, examining yourself, you can weep over the enormity of your faults.

THAIS. —If you hope that this could be useful to my salvation, I will not delay a moment in following your advice.

PAPHNUTIUS. — I have no doubt that this will be useful to your salvation.

THAIS. —Give me just a few moments to gather the riches that I have acquired so poorly and that I have possessed for too long.

PAPHNUTIUS. — Do not worry about your riches; there will be no shortage of people who will use them, once they have found them.

THAIS. — My intention, father, is neither to keep these goods nor to give them to my friends; I do not even think of distributing them to the natives, because I do not believe that the price of what must be expiated can be used in good works.

PAPHNUTIUS. - You are right; but what do you want to do with these heaps of wealth?

THAIS. — Deliver them to the flames and reduce them to ashes.

PAPHNUTIUS. - For what?

THAIS. — So as not to leave in the world what I could only acquire by sinning and insulting the Creator of the world.

PAPHNUTIUS. —Ah! how different you are from this Thaïs who formerly burned with impure passions and who was thirsty for gold [10]!

THAIS. —Perhaps I will become better, if it pleases God.

PAPHNUTIUS. — It is not difficult for its immutable essence to change all things; it is enough for him to want.

THAIS. — I am going to carry out my plan.

PAPHNUTIUS. — Go in peace and hasten to join me.

Scene IV.

THAIS, HER LOVERS.

THAIS. —Come here, run, all you fools, who have been my lovers!

THAI LOVERS. — It is the voice of Thaïs which calls us; let us hurry, let us not offend him by our slowness.

THAIS. — Come closer! come running! I have to exchange a few words with you.

THE LOVERS. — O Thaïs! Thaïs! What does this pyre that you are raising mean? Why do you pile up this miscellaneous pile of precious things there?

THAIS. — Are you asking for it?

THE LOVERS. —Your behavior strikes us as surprise.

THAIS. — I will explain it to you immediately.

THE LOVERS. — We beg you.

THAIS. - Look!

THE LOVERS. — Stop! stop, Thaïs! What are you doing? Have you lost your mind?

THAIS. — I didn't lose it; I recovered it!

THE LOVERS. —Why do you sacrifice four hundred pounds of gold and so much wealth of all kinds?

THAIS. — I want to consume in the flames everything that I have torn from you by evil actions, so that you cannot have the slightest hope of seeing me ever give in to your desires.

THE LOVERS. — Stop for a moment! stop! and tell us what is causing the trouble where you are.

THAIS. — I don't want to stay or talk to you any longer.

THE LOVERS. — Where do these disdains and this contempt come from? Are you accusing us of some infidelity? Have we not always satisfied your slightest desires? and now you are overwhelming us with unjust and motiveless hatred!

THAIS. — Leave me alone; do not tear my clothes to hold me back! Let it be enough for you that until this day I have sinned to please you. It's time to put an end to my mess. The time has come to part ways.

THE LOVERS. - Where are you going?

THAIS. — In a place where none of you will see me.

Scene V.

THAI LOVERS.

THE LOVERS. - Good Lord ! What is this miracle? Thaïs, our delights, she who only thought of immersing herself in luxury, she who never had any other thought than pleasure, and who had given herself over entirely to voluptuousness; now she sacrifices so much gold and precious stones without return! She despises us and suddenly deprives us of her presence!

Scene VI.

THAIS, PAPHNUCE.

THAIS. —Here I am, Paphnutius, my father! I come to you ready to obey you.

PAPHNUTIUS. — Your lateness was beginning to worry me. I feared that you had fallen back into the distractions of the century.

THAIS. — Do not be afraid: the thoughts that agitate me are very different. I disposed of my fortune as I wanted, and publicly renounced my lovers.

PAPHNUTIUS. — Since you have renounced them, you can now unite with your lover who is in heaven.

THAIS. — It is up to you to trace for me, as with a compass, the course of action I should take.

PAPHNUTIUS. - Follow me.

THAIS. — Would to God that I could follow you in my actions as well as in my walk!

Scene VII.

THE SAME.

PAPHNUTIUS. — You see this monastery. It is inhabited by a noble college of pious and holy virgins. This is where I want you to spend the time of your penance.

THAIS. — I cannot resist your will.

PAPHNUTIUS. — I am going to come in and ask the abbess, director of this house, to be kind enough to receive you there.

THAIS. —What should I do while waiting for you?

PAPHNUTIUS. - Come with me.

THAIS. — I will obey.

PAPHNUTIUS. — The abbess hastens to come and meet us. I don't understand who informed her so quickly of our arrival.

THAIS. — Fame, whose course no delay stops.

Scene VIII.

THE SAME, THE ABBEESS.

PAPHNUTIUS. — You come at the right time, illustrious abbess, it is you that I was looking for.

THE ABBESS. —You are most welcome, Paphnutius, our venerable father! Blessed be your arrival, you whom the Lord cherishes!

PAPHNUTIUS. — May the grace of the sovereign Creator shower upon you bliss and his eternal blessing!

THE ABBESS. — Where does this happiness come from, that your holiness deigns to visit my humble abode today?

PAPHNUTIUS. — I need your assistance in an urgent need.

THE ABBESS. —You just have to tell me, in one word, what you want; I will hasten to obey you and satisfy your wishes, as much as it is in my power.

PAPHNUTIUS. — I bring a half-dead goat that I have just snatched from the wolf's teeth; I ask you to grant her, to heal her, your merciful concern, until she has exchanged the rough skin of a goat for the soft fleece of a sheep.

THE ABBESS. — Explain yourself more clearly.

PAPHNUTIUS. — This woman you see led the life of a courtesan.

THE ABBESS. — This is deplorable.

PAPHNUTIUS. — She abandoned herself to all sensual pleasures.

THE ABBESS. — She lost herself.

PAPHNUTIUS. — But finally, by my advice, and with the help of Christ, she renounced the vanities which seduced her; obedient to my voice, she resolved to live chastely.

THE ABBESS. — Thanks be given to the author of this conversion!

PAPHNUTIUS. — Diseases of the soul, like those of the body, require the use of remedies. It is therefore necessary that this sinner, sequestered from the agitation common to secular people, be confined alone in a narrow cell where she can meditate at leisure on her faults.

THE ABBESS. — Nothing will be more useful to him.

PAPHNUTIUS. — Give orders for a cell to be built as soon as possible.

THE ABBESS. — She will be soon.

PAPHNUTIUS. — There must be no entry or exit; but only a small window through which she can receive the little food that you will give her on designated days and times.

THE ABBESS. — I fear that her delicacy cannot withstand the rigor of such a difficult life.

PAPHNUTIUS. — Don't worry. Such great faults need a proportionate remedy.

THE ABBESS. - It is true.

PAPHNUTIUS. — For me, what worries me are the delays; I cannot help but fear that this weak woman will fall back into the corrupt society of men.

THE ABBESS. —Why fear any longer? Why don't you contain it? The cell you requested is ready.

PAPHNUTIUS. — I am satisfied with it. Enter, Thaïs, into this cubbyhole, where you can properly mourn your troubles.

THAIS. — How narrow and dark this cell is! How inconvenient this stay is for a delicate woman!

PAPHNUTIUS. —Why do you curse this house? Why do you shudder to enter it? Untamed until this day, you have wandered without constraint; today it is appropriate that you receive a brake in solitude.

THAIS. — The soul accustomed to licentiousness cannot defend itself from a few weak returns to its past life.

PAPHNUTIUS. — This is why the reins of discipline must hold her back, until all revolt has ceased.

THAIS. — Degraded, as I am, I do not refuse to obey the orders of your fatherhood; but there is an inconvenience in this habitation which my weakness will bear with difficulty.

PAPHNUTIUS. - Which?

THAIS. — I blush to say it.

PAPHNUTIUS. — Don't blush; speak bluntly.

THAIS. — What is more painful, more revolting than being forced to satisfy all bodily necessities in the same place? It is certain that this cell will soon be infected and uninhabitable.

PAPHNUTIUS. — Fear eternal torments, and do not think of temporary inconveniences.

THAIS. —It is my weakness that forces me to fear.

PAPHNUTIUS. — You must atone through repulsive inconveniences for the guilty indolence and the delights in which you have lived.

THAIS. — I no longer resist: I agree that it is right that, soiled by impurity, I live in an impure and fetid pit. I only groan to see that there will be no place left for me where I can properly and decently invoke the name of the formidable majesty.

PAPHNUTIUS. —And where does this presumption come from? Would your defiled lips dare to pronounce the name of the spotless divinity?

THAIS. —And from whom can I hope for my forgiveness? Who will save me by his mercy, if I am forbidden to invoke him against whom I have sinned, and to whom alone I must offer my humble prayers?

PAPHNUTIUS. —You must pray not with your words, but with your tears, not by the plaintive sound of your voice, but by the inner rattle of your repentant heart.

THAIS. —If my voice is not permitted to pray to God, how can I hope for forgiveness?

PAPHNUTIUS. — You will obtain it all the more quickly the more you humiliate yourself. Only saySceneXi.: "O my Creator, have mercy on me! »

THAIS. — I really need him to have pity on me, so as not to be defeated in this perilous fight.

PAPHNUTIUS. —Fight with courage, and you will be victorious.

THAIS. — It is up to you, O my father, to pray for me to obtain the palm of victory.

PAPHNUTIUS. — This recommendation was not necessary.

THAIS. — I have hope. (*She enters the cell.*)

PAPHNUTIUS. — It is time for me to return to my solitude, and to see my beloved disciples again. Venerable abbess, I entrust this captive to your care and kindness. I ask you to give him what is necessary, without too much indulgence for his delicate body, and to regenerate his soul with your salutary exhortations.

THE ABBESS. — Don't worry, I will have the tenderness of a mother for her.

PAPHNUTIUS. - I must leave.

THE ABBESS. — Go in peace.

Scene IX.

PAPHNUCE, THE DISCIPLES.

A DISCIPLE. —Who is knocking at the door?

PAPHNUTIUS. - Me.

THE SAME DISCIPLES. — It's the voice of Paphnutius, our father!

PAPHNUTIUS. — Remove the lock.

THE DISCIPLES. — Hail, O our father!

PAPHNUTIUS. - Hi.

THE DISCIPLES. — The length of your absence worried us a lot.

PAPHNUTIUS. — I am glad I was absent.

THE DISCIPLES. —What happened to Thaïs?

PAPHNUTIUS. — What I wanted her to become.

THE DISCIPLES. — Where did you take her?

PAPHNUTIUS. — In a narrow cell, where she mourns her sins.

THE DISCIPLES. — Glory to the Holy Trinity!

PAPHNUTIUS. — Blessed be his awesome name, now and in all ages!

THE DISCIPLES. —Amen.

Scene X.

PAPHNUCE alone.

It has been three years [11] since Thaïs underwent her penance, and I do not know if her repentance is pleasing to God. I am going to go find my brother Antoine, so that, through his intervention, the truth becomes manifest to me.

Scene XI.

THE SAME, ANTOINE.

ANTHONY. — What unexpected happiness! what an unexpected source of joy! do I not see Paphnutius, my brother, my companion in solitude? It's himself.

PAPHNUTIUS. - It's me.

ANTHONY. — Welcome, my brother, your arrival fills me with joy.

PAPHNUTIUS. — I am no less satisfied to approach you than you are to receive me.

ANTHONY. — What event, so happy, so pleasant for us, brought you out of your retirement and brought you here?

PAPHNUTIUS. - I am going to tell you.

ANTHONY. - I wish.

PAPHNUTIUS. — More than three years ago, a courtesan named Thaïs came to settle in our neighborhood. Not only was she heading towards her ruin, but she was leading a crowd of lost souls to their deaths.

ANTHONY. - Oh! Deplorable disorder!

PAPHNUTIUS. — I went to find her under the guise of a lover. Sometimes I tried to bring back this heart given over to pleasure with gentle remonstrances, sometimes I frightened it with energetic advice and terrible threats.

ANTHONY. — This mixture was well suited to this type of weakness.

PAPHNUTIUS. — She finally gave in, and, renouncing her habits, she dedicated herself to chastity and consented to lock herself in a narrow cell.

ANTHONY. — What you teach me gives me so much satisfaction that every fiber of my heart trembles.

PAPHNUTIUS. — It is natural that your holiness rejoices, like me, in this conversion; but I am not without worry. I fear that this delicate woman had too much difficulty in enduring such a long and harsh penance.

ANTHONY. — True charity is always accompanied by pious compassion.

PAPHNUTIUS. — I ask you these feelings for Thaïs. Design, you and your disciples, to unite your prayers with mine, until a voice from heaven lets us know whether the tears of our penitent have softened and brought divine mercy to indulgence.

ANTHONY. — We wholeheartedly agree to your request.

PAPHNUTIUS. — God, in his mercy, will hear you, I am sure.

Scene XII.

THE SAME.

ANTHONY. — The evangelical promise has already been fulfilled in us.

PAPHNUTIUS. —What promise?

ANTHONY. — She said: 'Those who unite their prayers will obtain what they desire.'

PAPHNUTIUS. - What happened?

ANTHONY. — Paul my disciple has just had a vision.

PAPHNUTIUS. - Call him.

Scene XIII.

THE SAME, PAUL.

ANTHONY. — Paul, come closer, and tell Paphnutius what you saw.

PAUL. — I saw in the sky a magnificent bed, hung with white and which seemed to be guarded by four dazzling virgins. Admiring this astonishing splendor, I said to myself: So much glory belongs to no one as much as to my father and my master Antoine.

ANTHONY. — I don't believe myself worthy of such bliss.

PAUL. — Barely had I finished these words when a divine and thundering voice said to me: This glory is not, as you hope, reserved for Antoine, but for Thaïs, the courtesan!

PAPHNUTIUS. —Glory to your goodness! O Jesus, only son of God, who deigned to grant me this consolation in my sadness!

ANTHONY. — Let us praise the Lord; he is worthy of it.

PAPHNUTIUS. — I'm going to go see my captive.

ANTHONY. — The time has come when you can announce your forgiveness to her and console her with the promise of eternal bliss.

Scene XIV.

PAPHNUCE, THAIS.

PAPHNUTIUS. — Thais! my adopted daughter! Open your window for me, so that I can see you.

THAIS. - Who is talking to me?

PAPHNUTIUS. — Paphnutius, your father.

THAIS. — Where does this happiness come from that you deign to visit me, poor sinner?

PAPHNUTIUS. — Although for three years I have been physically absent, I have no less felt a constant solicitude for your salvation.

THAIS. - I have no doubt about it.

PAPHNUTIUS. — Tell me about the progress of your conversion and the progress of your repentance.

THAIS. — I can only tell you one thing; I know very well that I have done nothing that was worthy of the Lord.

PAPHNUTIUS. —If God examined all our iniquities, no conscience could support such an examination.

THAIS. — If, however, you want to know what I did: I gathered together, as if in a bundle, in my thoughts the multitude of my faults; I never stopped contemplating them and going over them in my mind. Also, as the foul odor of my cell did not leave my nostrils, so the fear of hell did not move away from the eyes of my conscience for a moment.

PAPHNUTIUS. — Because you punished yourself through repentance, you have deserved your forgiveness.

THAIS. — Would to heaven!

PAPHNUTIUS. — Give me your hand so I can help you out.

Thais. — O venerable father! Don't take this shit away from me. Defiled as I am, leave me in this place worthy of my merits.

Paphnutius. — The time has come to put aside fear and begin to hope for eternal life, for your penance has been pleasing to God.

Thais. — May all the angels praise his mercy, since he has not despised the humble repentance of a contrite heart!

Paphnutius. — Persist in the fear of God and in his love. When fifteen days have passed, you will strip off your human envelope, and, your pilgrimage being happily completed, you will return to your celestial homeland with the help of divine grace.

Thais. - Oh! May I escape the torments of hell, or at least be burned by less ardent flames, for it is not by my merits that I can obtain eternal bliss.

Paphnutius. — Divine grace does not weigh merit; because, if this free gift of divinity were only granted to merit, it would not be called grace.

Thais. — May the concert of heaven, may all the shrubs of the earth, may all species of animals, may the very chasms of lakes and seas unite to praise him who not only supports sinners, but who rewards with free favors to those who repent!

Paphnutius. — God has, and from all eternity, preferred mercy to punishment.

Thais. — Do not leave me, my venerable father; but stay close to me to console me at the hour when my body is about to dissolve.

Paphnutius. — I'm not going away; I only stand aside until the moment when your soul soars triumphantly towards heaven, I must deliver your body to the grave.

Scene XV.

THE SAME.

THAIS. — I'm starting to die.

PAPHNUTIUS. — Now is the time to pray.

THAIS. — You who created me, have pity on me and allow the soul you gave me to return happily to you.

PAPHNUTIUS. — O you who had no creator, truly immaterial being, whose simple essence formed from various parts the man who is not like you the one who is, allow that the elements of which this perishable creature is composed go to find the principle of their origin; that the soul, coming from heaven, participates in celestial joys, and that the body finds a fraternal and friendly layer in the bosom of the earth from which it came, until the day when this dust reunites and the breath of life reviving these members, this same Thaïs will rise again, a complete creature, as she was in her first life, to take her place among the white sheep of the Lord and enter into the joy of eternity; you who alone are he who is, you who reign in the unity of the Trinity and who are glorified for all ages! So be it.

The Scriptorium Project is the work of a small group of lay people of various apostolic churches who are interested in the preservation, transmission, and translation of the works of the early and medieval church. Our efforts are to make the works of the church fathers accessible to anyone who might have an interest in Christian antiquities and the theological, philosophical, and moral writings that have become the bedrock of Western Civilization.

To-date, our releases have pulled from the Greek, Syriac, Georgian, Latin, Celtic, Ethiopian, and Coptic traditions of Christianity, and have been pulled from sundry local traditions and languages.

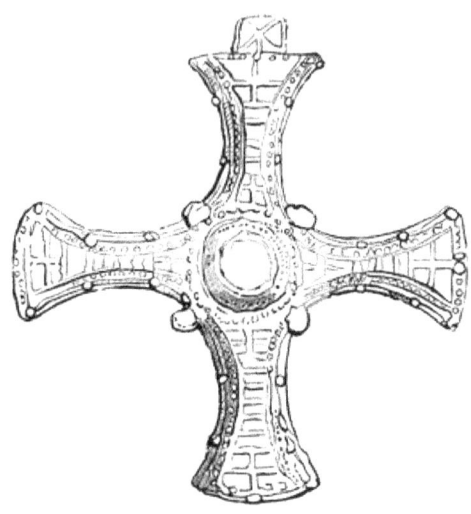

Other Selections from the Medieval German Church Series:

*Paphnutius & *Thaïs by Hrotsvitha of Gandersheim (June 2011)

Letters by Rudolf I Habsburg, Holy Roman Emperor (Dec. 2012)

About Fifteen Problems (De quindecim problematibus) by St. Albertus Magnus (Feb 2022)

On Fate (De Fato) by St. Albertus Magnus (Feb 2023)

www.ingramcontent.com/pod-product-compliance
Lightning Source LLC
LaVergne TN
LVHW052049070526
838201LV00086B/5153